GLO KOINONIA

The Sunrise On The Reaping

This book was professionally typeset on Reedsy.
Find out more at reedsy.com

Dedicated to y'all.

Contents

Preface

"Sunrise On The Reaping" is an immersive journey into a village bound by the mysterious rhythm of the land and the pulse that governs life itself. Mara, a young and perceptive guardian, rises to lead her people through the challenges of the reaping—a series of fissures that test courage, unity, and intuition. The book captures the delicate balance between human determination and the enduring forces of nature, offering readers a tale of suspense, growth, and profound connection to the earth.

Each fissure presents a unique trial, demanding more than skill; it calls for awareness, anticipation, and trust. Mara guides the villagers through these perilous encounters, teaching them not only to follow her lead but to feel the pulse of the land, to move in harmony with its rhythm, and to confront fear with collective courage. Through these tests, the community grows stronger, and Mara's bond with both the people and the land deepens, shaping her into a true guardian of the cycle.

The narrative unfolds across ten intense chapters, blending lyrical descriptions of nature with gripping tension as the fissures escalate in complexity. Shadows, energy, and unseen forces challenge the villagers' perception and resolve, creating a story that is both fantastical and deeply human. Readers are drawn into a world where every movement, every choice, and every connection matters, reflecting the delicate interplay of life, responsibility, and communion with the natural world.

Beyond the adventure and suspense, the story explores themes of leadership, unity, and self-discovery. Mara's journey is one of awakening—realizing that true guidance comes not from control but from connection, intuition, and trust. The villagers' transformation mirrors her own, showing that courage and harmony arise when individuals move together, guided by understanding, empathy, and shared purpose.

"Sunrise On The Reaping" is a tale that lingers long after the final page. It invites readers to reflect on the cycles that govern life, the unseen forces that shape our paths, and the power of unity in overcoming fear and adversity. With its rich, immersive storytelling and universal themes, this book promises to captivate readers seeking a story of adventure, suspense, and the profound beauty of human connection to the world around them.

Acknowledgments

All praise to Yahweh!

1

Chapter 1

The first light of dawn broke over the horizon with a quiet ferocity, painting the fields in shades of gold and crimson that made the morning seem almost sacred. Mist hovered over the earth like a delicate veil, and the air was heavy with the scent of dew and soil. The village lay in silence, not the soft, comforting kind of silence, but a tense one, as though every living thing knew something was about to change. Smoke curled lazily from the chimneys of small mud-brick houses, signaling the beginning of another day, yet the day felt different, charged with a sense of anticipation that pricked at the nerves of every inhabitant.

At the edge of the fields, where the tall grasses swayed like restless spirits, Mara crouched, her fingers gripping the rough handle of a sickle. Her eyes were fixed on the horizon, scanning for movement, though nothing yet stirred beyond the soft flutter of birds taking flight from the trees. Her heart hammered in her chest—not from exertion, but from fear, and from the knowledge that today was no ordinary day. Today marked the first sunrise of the reaping season, the moment when the village would pay its dues to the land, to the ancestors, to something older than memory itself. Her breath came in shallow bursts, and she tried to steady it, grounding herself with the smell of earth and the hum of cicadas that filled the air.

She was not alone. A few yards away, other villagers were emerging from their homes, their faces pale in the dawn light, carrying their own tools: sickles, scythes, baskets. Some walked silently, heads bowed, while others whispered prayers or muttered curses under their breath, as though hoping to deflect the attention of the unseen forces that demanded tribute. Mara's father, a man stooped with age but unyielding in presence, moved among them, nodding silently, murmuring instructions that sounded more like warnings than guidance. The reaping was a ritual older than the village itself, older than anyone could recount, yet no one dared question its authority. Those who had, long ago, were gone, swallowed by the unforgiving cycles of the harvest that seemed to choose its victims as much as its yield.

The sun rose further, stretching its first fingers of light across the fields, glinting off the dew in a way that made the grass seem like a sea of molten gold. Mara shifted, letting her gaze fall upon the rows of wheat that had been planted months before, their heads heavy with grain. Normally, she would have felt pride at the sight, the promise of nourishment and survival, but now the wheat seemed to sway with a life of its own, whispering warnings that only she could hear. She remembered the stories her grandmother told, tales of villagers who had vanished during the reaping, claimed by the fields themselves when the moon had hung full and bright and the harvesters had been careless.

2

Mara's stomach knotted, and she tightened her grip on the sickle. The sharp metal felt reassuring, even if it was nothing compared to the forces she sensed gathering beyond the treeline.

From the forest, a low rustle announced the arrival of the first riders. They emerged slowly, spectral in the morning haze, cloaked in fabrics of deep blue and gray that flickered like shadows. Their horses were black as midnight, eyes glinting with an almost unnatural intelligence. Mara had never seen them before in the village. They were not traders, nor soldiers, nor messengers. They were something else entirely, and their presence made her skin crawl. Her father's voice came beside her, low and urgent. "Stay close. Do not speak unless spoken to." His eyes followed the riders with a mixture of reverence and dread. "They mark the beginning."

The villagers lined up, a hesitant procession moving toward the heart of the fields where the wheat grew thickest. Mara joined them, her steps careful, trying to avoid the slippery patches of dew-soaked earth. The riders had stopped at the edge of the first row, their leader dismounting silently, boots sinking into the soil with a sound that seemed too deliberate to be ordinary. He wore a hood, shadows concealing his face, but Mara felt his gaze, sharp and piercing, sweeping over the villagers as though weighing each soul. A chill ran through her, and she found herself wishing for the comfort of her grandmother's stories, even if those stories ended in disappearance and despair. There was something comforting about known dangers.

The leader lifted a hand, and the village fell utterly silent, as if the sound of breathing itself might offend him. He spoke,

3

his voice deep and resonant, carrying across the fields without the need for shouting. "The reaping begins," he said. The words seemed to echo from the trees, reverberating in Mara's chest. She swallowed, feeling the familiar tremor of fear and anticipation. She had been prepared for this day, yet preparation felt meaningless now in the presence of those who came to enforce it.

With a swift motion, the rider drew a blade, long and curved, catching the sunlight in a gleam that made it seem as though fire had been trapped within the metal. Mara's father stepped forward instinctively, raising his hands in supplication. The rider did not strike, only watched, and then turned toward the fields. The villagers followed him, moving in step with an almost hypnotic precision, guided by the silent authority of the riders. Mara's legs moved on their own, carrying her into the wheat, the sickle in her hand suddenly feeling insignificant.

The wheat seemed to shift around them as they walked, whispering and rustling in a language Mara could almost understand. The sun climbed higher, burning away the morning mist, revealing the full expanse of the fields. It was more than crops, more than nourishment—it was a living thing, breathing, watching, waiting. Mara glanced at the villagers around her, noting the tension etched into every line of their bodies. Some had eyes wide with awe, some with fear, and a few were already muttering prayers under their breath. The ritual was not simply about harvesting wheat. It was about acknowledging a presence, a power that demanded recognition and respect. And today, Mara felt, it hung closer than ever, tangible in the warmth of the sun and the chill of the shadows.

4

By mid-morning, the work had begun. Sickles flashed, slicing through stalks of wheat with a rhythm that was both beautiful and terrifying. Mara moved with practiced efficiency, her hands steady despite the fear gnawing at her chest. The riders remained at the edge, silent sentinels, watching, occasionally nodding to the villagers as though approving their efforts—or condemning them. Every cut of wheat sent a shiver through Mara, as though the land itself were alive and responding to her touch. She had heard the old stories about those who had harvested poorly, who had ignored the rhythm of the reaping and had been claimed in the night. She did not dare falter.

As the sun reached its zenith, a sudden shift in the air drew Mara's attention. The wheat ahead of her began to shimmer, not with dew or sunlight, but with something else, an almost liquid glow that pulsed as though alive. Mara froze, heart hammering. The rider leader stepped forward again, raising his blade, not in threat, but in acknowledgment. The villagers paused mid-cut, eyes wide. The wheat parted, revealing a narrow path that had not been there before, winding deep into the fields like a vein of light through the earth. Mara felt an irresistible pull toward it, a compulsion she could not name. Her father placed a hand on her shoulder, grounding her. "Do not stray," he warned, voice tight with tension. "The path chooses whom it will."

The hours passed, each one dragging and surging at the same time. The villagers continued their work, and the path persisted, glowing softly, almost beckoning. Mara found herself glancing at it constantly, feeling a growing unease mixed with fascination. The sun moved slowly across the sky, shadows stretching long as afternoon approached. And then, as if sensing the peak of the day, the riders stirred. The leader raised his hand once more, and the villagers paused, waiting. He spoke again, and this time his words were a chant, low and rhythmic, carrying an ancient cadence that resonated with the very soil beneath their feet.

The ground trembled, subtle at first, then stronger. Mara stumbled, clutching her sickle, eyes wide with fear. The wheat around the path swayed violently, parting further to reveal the earth beneath, dark and moist, as though breathing. A low hum rose from the soil itself, vibrating through Mara's bones. She glanced at her father, who had gone pale, hands gripping his staff as though it were the only thing holding him in place. The villagers around her were silent now, eyes fixed on the center of the field where the path led, all waiting for what was to come.

And then, with a sound like the tearing of the world itself, the earth cracked along the path. Light poured from the fissure, blinding, golden and pure, filling the fields with a radiance that made the wheat gleam like molten metal. Mara fell to her knees, shielding her eyes. The riders moved closer, silent as shadows, and from the fissure came a wind, strong and commanding, carrying a scent of flowers and smoke, of old wood and rain-soaked earth. Mara could feel it seeping into her skin, into her very bones, and she knew that the reaping had begun in earnest. This was no longer merely cutting wheat. This was a confrontation with something primeval, something that had always been part of the village but had remained hidden, patient, waiting for the moment of release.

Voices rose among the villagers, some in fear, some in awe, and some in prayer. Mara's father lifted his hands again, and she could see his lips moving, forming words that were more instinct than thought, a language that had been passed down through generations. Mara joined him, her voice shaking at first, then stronger, resonating with the chant that seemed to connect them to the very core of the earth. The fissure widened, light spilling over, and the wind wrapped around the villagers, tugging at their hair, their clothes, their very spirits.

Mara could feel it calling her, a summons she could neither resist nor fully understand. The sickle in her hand felt weightless now, a mere token of something greater. She knew, deep down, that the reaping was not just a harvest—it was a reckoning. The village, the land, the unseen forces—they were all entwined in a cycle older than memory, and the first sunrise of the reaping was only the beginning. Whatever lay ahead would change everything, leaving nothing untouched. The glow of the fissure reflected in her eyes, and Mara understood, with a clarity that terrified her, that the path would claim what it would, and survival would demand more than courage. It would demand surrender, understanding, and perhaps something even deeper: the willingness to embrace what the dawn itself had to offer, even if it meant losing the world she had always known.

The villagers, too, were caught in the revelation, their chants mingling with the hum of the earth, creating a harmony that was both beautiful and unsettling. Mara felt her body responding to the rhythm, moving almost of its own accord, stepping closer to the path, drawn by a force beyond reason. The riders stood as witnesses, their presence solemn, almost ceremonial. The leader lowered his blade, signaling the moment had fully come. And as Mara's foot crossed the threshold of the glowing path, a shiver ran through her, a mixture of fear, awe, and anticipation. The wheat whispered around her, and for a fleeting second, she thought she heard her name, carried on the wind, mingling with the scent of the earth and the song of the dawn.

She stepped forward again, deeper into the unknown, leaving behind the familiar fields, the trembling villagers, and the safety of the sunlit earth. The path wound ahead, pulsing, alive, and Mara knew without doubt that the reaping had truly begun. What waited at the end of the path, what judgment or revelation, she could not yet see, but the certainty of it filled her with a strange exhilaration. The first sunrise on the reaping was not merely the start of the harvest—it was the awakening of forces older than the village itself, and Mara, trembling yet unyielding, would face them, for she was bound to the land, to the dawn, and to the reckoning that had finally arrived.

The villagers behind her continued their chant, their voices rising and falling with the rhythm of the wind. The riders remained silent, motionless, shadows against the brilliant light. Mara's heart thrummed in time with the pulsing glow beneath her feet, a reminder that life, death, and the cycle of the harvest were not separate, but intertwined. The path stretched onward, promising challenges and revelations, and Mara, gripping her sickle, felt the weight of destiny settle upon her shoulders. Each step she took carried her further from innocence and deeper into the mystery that had long haunted the edges of her world. The sunrise had come, and with it, the beginning of everything.

2

Chapter 2

The light from the fissure in the wheat fields lingered long after Mara had stepped onto the path, painting the morning sky in hues of gold and crimson that seemed unnatural, almost otherworldly. She moved cautiously, every sense heightened, aware of the whispering wheat and the distant hum that vibrated through the soil beneath her feet. The path stretched ahead, winding through the fields, glowing faintly with a life of its own, as if it knew the rhythm of her heartbeat and matched it with each pulse of light. Behind her, the villagers' chants faded into a murmur, swallowed by the distance and the overwhelming presence of the path. The riders remained at the edge, shadows against the bright fissure, their eyes unreadable, like statues carved from night itself.

Mara walked in silence, her sickle held loosely at her side. Each step felt heavier than the last, though there was no weight to the air. The path seemed endless, bending and turning in ways that made the horizon impossible to gauge. The wheat on either side shimmered as though alive, bending toward her in gentle waves, whispering secrets she could almost comprehend. She shivered, a mixture of fear and awe tightening her chest. The stories her grandmother had told about the reaping flooded her mind—the vanished villagers, the whispering wheat, the unseen power that demanded tribute. She had dismissed them as old tales meant to scare children. Now, every word seemed tangible, real, and immediate.

As she moved deeper into the glowing corridor, the air changed. The scent of earth and dew gave way to something sweeter, sharper, a mix of flowers and smoke, like incense burning over a sacred altar. Mara's senses tingled. The temperature shifted too, neither warm nor cold, but a strange in-between that made the hairs on her arms stand on end. The path seemed to pulse beneath her feet, and she realized she could feel the vibration of something immense moving far below the surface, a heartbeat of the land itself. She stumbled once, catching herself against the stalks of wheat, and felt a sudden compulsion to look down into the glowing soil. It seemed almost liquid, swirling with light, as if the earth itself were breathing. Her reflection shimmered back at her, distorted and flickering, her eyes wide with the realization that she was no longer merely a villager walking through a field. She was part of something larger, something older.

The path began to narrow, the wheat closing in, tall stalks brushing against her arms. The whispers grew louder, no longer merely rustling sounds, but almost words, fragmented and fleeting. Mara caught snippets, phrases that seemed familiar yet incomprehensible: "The chosen walks...," "The harvest calls...," "The sun will judge..." Her heart raced. She felt a pull forward, magnetic, as though the path itself were urging her to move faster, to leave hesitation behind. She took a deep breath and pressed onward, ignoring the tremor in her legs.

Suddenly, the path opened into a clearing. The wheat ended abruptly, replaced by a patch of bare earth that glowed with a strange golden light, radiating from a pit at its center. The pit was not deep, yet it seemed to go down forever, a bottomless well of shimmering energy. Mara stepped closer, unable to resist the compulsion to look, and felt a warmth wash over her, seeping into her chest, filling her lungs. Her reflection in the surface of the pit was no longer hers alone. It flickered and multiplied, images of herself in different poses, different ages, even different emotions she had never experienced. She felt dizzy, almost sick, but the vision persisted, compelling her to stare, to understand.

A voice broke through the hum, low and resonant, though it came from no visible source. "Mara." Her name sounded foreign in the air, echoing, vibrating. "You have come as the first sunrise demanded. You will see what the reaping requires." She swallowed hard, her throat dry. "Who... who are you?" she whispered, though the voice had no mouth, no form. "I am what has always been here," the voice replied. "I am the cycle, the harvest, the keeper of what is given and taken. You are chosen to witness, to understand, to endure." The ground beneath her shifted slightly, and the pit pulsed in response, as if in affirmation.

Mara took a step back, fear twisting in her stomach. She felt the instinct to flee, to return to the safety of the village and the familiar sunlit fields, but her feet remained rooted. The pull of the path, of the pit, was stronger than fear. She lowered her sickle and let her hands hang by her sides. The voice spoke again, this time softer, almost tender. "Do not fear what is necessary. The reaping is balance. Life and death are one, and you stand at the threshold." The air around her seemed to thrum with energy, vibrating in harmony with her own heartbeat. She realized with a shock that she could feel the wheat beyond the clearing responding, bending slightly toward the pit, shimmering more brightly. It was as though the land itself was aware of her presence, acknowledging her passage.

A sudden movement at the edge of the clearing made her glance up. The riders had followed, silent and solemn, dismounting without a sound. Their horses pawed at the earth, but they did not stray from the edge. The leader stepped forward, hood still concealing his face, and inclined his head toward the pit. Mara felt a wave of recognition, though she had never seen him before. "You are ready," he said simply. No explanation, no instruction, only certainty. Mara nodded slowly, unsure if she was agreeing or merely complying with the invisible force that guided her steps.

The rider extended a hand, and Mara hesitated, then took it. The moment their skin met, the warmth of the pit seemed to surge through her veins. Images flashed in her mind: the cycles of seasons, the faces of those who had been reaped before her, the laughter and tears of villagers long gone, and the endless rhythm of sun and earth and life. She saw herself in every moment of the harvest, in every hand that had touched the soil, every prayer uttered into the wind. She felt connected, as though she were not merely a participant but a conduit, a vessel through which the history and future of the village passed.

Time lost meaning. The sun rose higher, casting its full light over the clearing, but the glow from the pit never dimmed. Mara knelt beside it, watching the swirling energy. The voice spoke again, quieter now, almost a whisper of wind. "You must take the first cut. Not of wheat, but of the cycle itself. Only then will the reaping be honored." Her hand shook as she lifted the sickle. She looked at the pit, then at the leader, then at the wheat that had followed her into this space, shimmering like liquid gold. She raised the blade, and for a moment, everything seemed to hold its breath. The wind stilled, the hum of the earth softened, and the wheat froze in mid-sway.

The cut came, almost by instinct. She slashed the sickle through the air and felt the energy of the pit respond, a surge of warmth and light that enveloped her entirely. The ground beneath her feet seemed to ripple, and for a heartbeat, she felt herself lifted, floating above the earth. The whispers of the wheat became voices, clear now, speaking in a chorus that resonated within her chest: "Balance... life... death... the harvest continues..." Mara gasped, falling to her knees, but the energy did not leave her. She felt it flow through her, through every cell, every thought, binding her to the land, to the cycle, to the reaping.

When she opened her eyes again, the clearing was unchanged, yet everything felt different. The wheat swayed gently, no longer whispering threats, but acknowledging her presence. The pit pulsed softly, its light more serene than before, as though satisfied with the first offering. The riders remained silent, their presence heavy with approval, yet they did not speak. Mara realized that the burden of the reaping was not theirs to bear. It was hers, hers alone, as well as those who had been chosen before and would be chosen again.

Her father emerged from the path, pale and trembling, but relief and pride mingling in his eyes. "You... you have done it," he whispered, voice cracking. Mara nodded slowly, still over-whelmed, still processing the enormity of what had occurred. She felt the energy of the pit settling into her, a quiet resonance that seemed to anchor her to the world, yet simultaneously open her to possibilities she could not yet comprehend. The riders mounted silently, turning back toward the edge of the fields, their horses moving like shadows against the golden light. They would remain at the borders, guardians of the cycle, until the next sunrise demanded their presence.

The villagers began to return, moving cautiously, eyes wide with awe. Some avoided looking at Mara, sensing that she had changed, that she had crossed a threshold invisible to those who had stayed behind. Others whispered her name, awe and fear mixed in their tones, recognizing the gravity of what had occurred. Mara stood slowly, still feeling the pulse of the pit within her veins. She looked at her father, who placed a hand on her shoulder, grounding her once more. "You have begun what others could not," he said quietly. "The reaping continues, but you have taken the first step. Remember this, child: the sun rises for all, but not all rise with it."

As the day drew on, Mara walked back along the glowing path, now dimming in the bright sunlight, guiding herself with memory and instinct. The wheat returned to its normal sway, the whispers fading into the rustle of the wind. She felt the weight of what had been given, what had been demanded, and what had been endured. Her eyes were open to the unseen forces of the land, her mind attuned to the rhythm of life and death, harvest and sacrifice. She knew the reaping would continue for months, seasons, perhaps lifetimes, yet she also knew that she had been marked, chosen, and bound to its cycle in ways that would shape her forever.

By the time she reached the village, the sun hung high in the sky, bathing the fields in a warm, steady light. The villagers greeted her cautiously, their reverence clear, their fear tempered by hope. Mara felt their eyes on her, measuring, questioning, understanding. She lowered her sickle, the weight of it familiar now, a reminder that tools alone could not define the reaping—only courage, understanding, and connection to the forces that governed life and death could.

As Mara stepped into the first house she saw, the shadows of the riders faded in the distance, leaving only the hum of the village and the whisper of wheat beyond the fields. She knew the cycle had begun anew, and with it, her life had irrevocably changed. The first sunrise of the reaping had not merely marked the start of a harvest—it had awakened something ancient, something powerful, something that would demand her attention, her strength, and her spirit in the days to come. And Mara, heart pounding, yet steady, understood that this was only the beginning.

3

Chapter 3

The evening descended slowly over the village, stretching shadows across the mud-brick houses and the fields that now seemed ordinary in the fading light. Yet Mara knew better. She had crossed the threshold that the first sunrise of the reaping had opened, and nothing would ever look the same again. The glow from the path had vanished with the midday sun, leaving only a faint hum beneath the earth that Mara could feel in her bones if she paused long enough to listen. She walked through the village, her footsteps careful, her eyes scanning familiar faces for signs of recognition or fear. The villagers had returned to their homes, murmuring prayers of thanks and relief, but she sensed in them a mixture of awe and unease, a silent acknowledgment that she had done what no one else had dared.

Her father met her at the doorway of their home, his eyes reflecting both pride and apprehension. "You have seen it, haven't you?" he asked quietly, voice carrying the weight of unspoken questions. Mara nodded. "I have," she said. Her voice was steady, though her hands trembled slightly from the lingering energy of the pit. "It is alive... and it watches."

Her father sighed, leading her inside. The room smelled of smoke and herbs, familiar and grounding, yet Mara felt the contrast sharply—the normalcy of home against the extraordinary she had witnessed. "The reaping is more than wheat," he said slowly, settling onto a wooden stool. "It is balance, life and death intertwined. Few ever understand it. Fewer still survive it with clarity." Mara sank to the floor beside him, feeling the solidity of the earth beneath her, the hum in her veins quieting to a gentle rhythm.

Night fell fully, and the village seemed to exhale, the tension of the day slowly dissipating into the cool air. Lanterns glimmered softly in windows, smoke curled lazily from chimneys, and the low chatter of families settling in for the evening filled the quiet streets. Mara, however, could not rest. The memory of the pit, the shimmering path, and the pull she had felt lingered in her mind, refusing to fade. She stepped outside once more, drawn to the edge of the fields where the first sunrise had changed everything. The wheat rustled softly in the night breeze, a gentle murmur that seemed almost affectionate compared to the voices that had demanded attention earlier.

She knelt at the edge of the field, running her hands over the cool stalks. The hum beneath the soil was faint but persistent, a heartbeat she could feel more than hear. It reminded her that the reaping was not complete; it was a cycle that demanded attention, respect, and participation. The first sunrise had been a beginning, not an end. Mara closed her eyes, letting her senses absorb the quiet power of the night. Somewhere in the distance, a wolf howled, and she felt the connection, faint yet undeniable, between the creatures of the land and the unseen forces that guided the harvest.

A sudden rustle behind her made her start. She turned, hand gripping her sickle instinctively, but it was only a figure emerging from the shadows of the village. One of the riders, hooded and silent, approached, the horse he led moving soundlessly over the damp earth. Mara rose to her feet, a mixture of fear and recognition tightening her chest. The rider stopped a few paces away, bowing slightly. "The cycle stirs," he said, voice low, carrying the resonance of authority and time. "You have taken the first step, Mara. But the harvest is far from complete."

Mara swallowed, feeling the weight of the words. "What must I do?" she asked, though she suspected the answer would not be simple.

The rider extended a hand, and Mara saw a faint glow emanating from his fingertips, the light gentle yet impossible to ignore. "You must learn the rhythm," he said. "The land has a heartbeat. The wheat, the soil, even the wind—they are connected. The reaping chooses not merely what is harvested, but who participates. Tonight, you will feel the pulse of the harvest, and it will teach you what your hands must do tomorrow."

He turned, leading her toward the path that had vanished with the sunset, now marked only by the faint shimmer of dew and the hum of the earth. Mara followed, her heart pounding, every sense alert. The night air was cool, carrying the scent of wet soil and wildflowers, and the darkness seemed to thrum with life. As they reached the edge of the field, the rider stopped and gestured toward a hollow where the earth seemed to pulse faintly, a shadow of the pit she had seen earlier. Mara knelt beside it, hands hovering above the soil.

The rider spoke again, chanting in a language she did not know but somehow understood. The hum beneath her hands grew stronger, rising into a resonance that vibrated through her entire body. Images flashed before her eyes: the planting of seeds, the growth of stalks, the care of soil, the taking of life for sustenance, the faces of villagers from generations past, and the hands that had harvested before hers. Each image carried a lesson, subtle yet profound. Mara realized she was not merely observing; she was participating, her mind and body absorbing the rhythm, the cadence, the balance required to honor the reaping.

Hours seemed to pass in moments. The rider remained beside her, silent, guiding without touching, allowing her to discover the rhythm for herself. The hum in the soil became a song, one that Mara felt in her chest, in her limbs, in the tips of her fingers. She moved her hands over the earth, tracing the invisible currents of energy, feeling the subtle shifts that indicated where life was strong, where decay threatened, where the harvest demanded care. Sweat dampened her brow, though the air was cool, and she realized she had not noticed the passing of time, absorbed entirely in the communion with the land.

When she finally looked up, the first hints of dawn were brushing the horizon, the stars fading into pale streaks of light. The rider stepped back, bowing once more. "The sun rises again," he said, voice low but resonant. "The village awaits. The first day of the harvest has begun, and you will lead. Remember the rhythm. Follow the pulse. Honor the cycle, and it will honor you." Mara nodded, understanding that the ritual of the night had been preparation, an awakening of senses and awareness that would guide her actions in the day to come.

She returned to the village as the first golden rays touched the rooftops, moving with a quiet confidence that had not been there the day before. Villagers were stirring, gathering tools, murmuring prayers, and watching her with a mixture of hope and fear. Mara's father met her at the edge of the fields, eyes wide. "You... you have changed," he said. Mara nodded, letting her hands fall to her sides. "I have learned," she replied simply.

The villagers followed her into the fields, their movements cautious but synchronized, trusting her guidance even as they sensed the power she now carried. Mara moved among them, demonstrating the proper way to cut the wheat, how to feel the rhythm of the land beneath their feet, how to respect the life they were taking. Some hesitated, uncertain, but Mara's confidence was infectious. The sun rose higher, painting the fields in the familiar golden hue, yet every stalk of wheat seemed charged with the memory of the night, shimmering faintly in response to her presence.

Hours passed in quiet labor. The rhythm Mara had felt in the hollow beneath the earth now guided her movements, and she could sense the land responding. The wheat seemed to bend slightly as she approached, guiding her cuts, whispering directions in the faint hum that only she could hear. Villagers began to follow instinctively, learning to feel the pulse as she did, their movements becoming more fluid, more deliberate. The harvest proceeded not merely as a task, but as a communion, a shared awareness of the life they took and the balance they maintained.

By midday, Mara felt a shift. The hum in the earth had intensified, and the wind carried a new scent, sharp and electrifying. Clouds gathered faintly on the horizon, though the sun remained bright. She paused, hand resting on the hilt of her sickle, feeling the energy ripple through the fields. Something was coming. She could sense it, a presence both powerful and deliberate, moving toward them. The villagers noticed as well, their motions slowing, eyes widening, whispering among themselves. Mara turned, scanning the horizon, and saw a second fissure forming, smaller than the first but no less ominous, glowing faintly as though the earth itself were breathing it into existence.

The rider appeared at her side, voice calm but commanding. "The balance shifts. Another will rise to challenge the harmony. You must be ready." Mara's heart raced, but she felt a quiet determination settle within her. "What must I do?" she asked.

"Observe," he replied. "Learn. Guide. Protect. The cycle demands understanding more than strength, wisdom more than courage. You will not face it alone, but your hand will shape the outcome. Remember the rhythm. Follow the pulse. Honor the cycle."

Mara nodded again, gripping her sickle firmly. She felt the energy in the fields pulse in time with her heartbeat, a steady rhythm that grounded her, sharpened her senses, and prepared her for what was to come. The villagers around her looked to her for guidance, trusting in the authority the reaping had bestowed. The second fissure glowed brighter, and Mara understood that the true challenge of the harvest had only begun.

She stepped forward, feeling the hum of the earth beneath her feet, the whispers of the wheat around her, and the gaze of unseen forces upon her. The first sunrise had awakened her, the night had prepared her, and now the day demanded her full attention. The reaping was no longer merely a task or a ritual— it was an awakening, a test, and a responsibility that she would bear, shaping the life of her village and the balance of the land itself. Mara lifted her sickle once more, heart steady, mind clear, and stepped toward the glowing fissure, ready to face whatever the land required of her next.

4

Chapter 4

The sun climbed higher over the village, burning away the last vestiges of morning mist and painting the fields in brilliant gold. Mara moved through the wheat with a sense of purpose now, her every motion guided by the rhythm she had learned during the night beneath the glowing hollow. The villagers followed, their movements cautious but synchronized, their eyes occasionally flicking toward her for guidance. The energy of the land pulsed faintly beneath their feet, a silent song that Mara felt more than heard, each beat resonating with her own heartbeat. Today, the harvest felt alive in a way it never had before, as though the wheat itself were conscious, aware of the reverence with which it was being treated.

She stopped for a moment, scanning the rows of stalks that stretched endlessly before her. The second fissure, which had appeared at the edge of the field yesterday, glowed faintly, its light pulsing in tandem with the hum beneath the earth. Mara felt its pull, subtle but insistent, tugging at her mind, drawing her toward it as though it demanded her attention. She knew the villagers could sense it too, though they dared not approach it. Their fear was palpable, and yet there was a curiosity beneath it, a silent recognition that this was no ordinary harvest. Mara lifted her hand, signaling them to continue their work, and they obeyed, cutting the wheat in careful, precise strokes, their movements almost reverent.

The rider who had guided her during the night appeared at the edge of the field, moving with the same silent grace she had come to associate with his presence. His horse stepped lightly over the soil, hooves barely touching the ground, and he inclined his head toward Mara. "The cycle shifts," he said, his voice low, carrying the weight of time and authority. "You have mastered the rhythm of the first cut, but the land will demand more. The second fissure will test you, and through it, the village."

Mara nodded, feeling the familiar surge of energy in her veins. She gripped her sickle tightly, letting the hum beneath her feet guide her steps. She approached the second fissure slowly, feeling the wheat bend slightly as she passed, whispering encouragement or warning—she could not tell which. The glow of the fissure intensified as she drew near, golden light rippling across the soil as though responding to her presence. She knelt at the edge, placing a hand on the earth, and felt a pulse that was stronger, more insistent than the first. Images flashed through her mind: the cycles of growth and decay, the hands of villagers past and present, the lives intertwined with the land, and the choices that shaped the balance of harvest and life.

A sudden voice broke through the hum, resonant and commanding. "Mara." It was different from the voice she had heard before, colder, sharper, and carrying a sense of urgency. "The harvest must not falter. You must guide them." Mara lifted her head, scanning the fissure. Shadows moved within the glow, shapes indistinct but alive, shifting and writhing like smoke in the wind. She felt a surge of fear, but it was tempered by understanding—the fissure demanded attention, demanded her leadership, demanded the village's participation in a way she had not yet experienced.

The villagers, sensing the change in energy, paused in their work, eyes wide and hesitant. Mara rose to her feet, raising her sickle high. "Do not fear," she called, voice steady, carrying over the rustling wheat. "Follow the rhythm. Trust the land. Trust yourselves." Her words were met with silence, then tentative nods as the villagers resumed their work, guided by her calm authority. The hum of the earth beneath them grew louder, a steady pulse that seemed to synchronize the movements of every hand in the field.

The shadows in the fissure began to solidify, forming figures that emerged slowly, rising from the glowing pit like spirits called forth by the harvest. Mara's stomach tightened. They were not hostile, but neither were they benign. Their presence radiated power, ancient and inscrutable, and she felt the weight of their attention upon her. The rider stepped beside her, silent as always, and placed a hand lightly on her shoulder. "They are part of the cycle," he said. "Not enemies, not allies. They exist to ensure the balance is maintained. Respect them, and the harvest will continue. Challenge them, and the land itself may turn against you."

Mara nodded, heart hammering, and stepped closer to the fissure. The figures within the glow shifted in response to her approach, circling slowly, their movements deliberate and mesmerizing. She raised her sickle, not in aggression but as a symbol of participation, acknowledging the power and authority they embodied. One of the figures moved forward, larger than the others, its form flickering like liquid light. It extended a hand, and Mara felt a pull, not physical but spiritual, drawing her attention, testing her resolve. She held her ground, letting the rhythm of the land guide her, letting the hum beneath her feet anchor her in place.

The figure spoke without words, projecting images and sensations directly into her mind. Mara saw the consequences of carelessness, the balance of life and death tipping, the village faltering under neglect, the wheat withering and the soil becoming barren. Then she saw the reverse: hands guided by understanding, movements in harmony with the earth, the harvest thriving, the village prospering, and the cycle maintained. She understood immediately—the fissure was a test, a challenge to ensure that she could lead the village in honoring the harvest without faltering.

Mara exhaled, feeling a mixture of fear and determination. She lifted her sickle and moved closer to the fissure, placing her hands on the glowing soil. The energy surged through her, coursing into her veins, and she felt a connection stronger than anything she had experienced before. The hum beneath her feet became a song, harmonizing with the whispers of the wheat and the subtle movements of the figures in the fissure. She guided the villagers with precise instructions, moving among them, adjusting their angles, their strokes, their timing. The wheat responded, swaying and bending as though alive, the rhythm of the harvest syncing perfectly with her own heartbeat.

Hours passed in a blur of motion and focus. The figures in the fissure circled, watching, testing, observing Mara's every action. She felt their approval when she maintained balance, their subtle warnings when she faltered even slightly. The villagers, guided by her and the unseen hands of the fissure, moved in perfect harmony, their work becoming both labor and ritual. The sun arced across the sky, and Mara scarcely noticed its passage, absorbed entirely in the communion with the land and the forces that governed it.

By mid-afternoon, the second fissure had begun to shrink, its glow dimming as the villagers continued their work in rhythm. Mara felt a sense of accomplishment, though tempered by exhaustion. The energy of the land had been generous, but it demanded vigilance and respect. She glanced at the rider, who remained at the edge, silent and observing. He inclined his head slightly, an acknowledgment of her success, but said nothing. Mara understood—this was her achievement, and the cycle had recognized her.

The villagers began to tire, their movements slowing, but Mara guided them gently, helping maintain the rhythm without forcing it. The hum beneath the earth softened, becoming a gentle undertone rather than a pulsing command. The wheat seemed to sway with satisfaction, whispering softly as the glow of the fissure faded completely. Mara felt the exhaustion in her limbs, but also a profound sense of connection, a quiet satisfaction that transcended fatigue. The harvest had been honored, the cycle maintained, and the village had participated fully under her guidance.

As the sun began its descent toward the horizon, Mara walked to the center of the field, kneeling once more on the earth. She placed her hands on the soil, feeling the gentle hum, the whispers of the wheat, and the lingering presence of the figures that had risen from the fissure. The energy was no longer overwhelming, but calm and steady, a reminder that the land's power was constant, patient, and eternal. She closed her eyes, letting the sensations wash over her, absorbing the lessons of the day and the night that had preceded it.

Her father approached quietly, placing a hand on her shoulder. "You have done well," he said, voice soft but carrying pride. "The village will remember this day, and the land will remember you. The reaping is not complete, but you have guided the first challenge with wisdom and courage." Mara opened her eyes, meeting his gaze. She nodded, understanding the weight of his words. The reaping was ongoing, a cycle that would continue beyond her lifetime, yet she had taken her place within it, marked by the first sunrise and solidified by the events of this day.

Night fell again, and the village settled into a quiet routine. Mara walked slowly through the fields, the wheat swaying gently in the cool breeze, whispering their secrets softly now. The first fissure had closed completely, the second had been absorbed into the earth, leaving only memory and the faint hum beneath the soil. She felt the energy settle within her, a quiet pulse that would guide her in the days to come. The rider remained at the edge of the fields, watching silently, a reminder that the unseen forces of the reaping were ever-present, patient and vigilant.

Mara returned to her home, exhausted but alert, her mind racing with the events of the day. She sat beside her father, recounting the experience in fragmented words, feeling the energy of the fields lingering in her veins. He listened quietly, nodding, understanding more than she could articulate. The village would sleep, resting in the normalcy of the night, but Mara knew the truth: the reaping had awakened forces older than the village, and her role within it was only beginning. She felt a mixture of fear, determination, and anticipation—a readiness for whatever challenges lay ahead, a willingness to honor the rhythm and follow the pulse, and the understanding that the balance of life, death, and harvest rested in part upon her hands.

The stars emerged in the night sky, glittering above the village with indifferent beauty. Mara stepped outside once more, gazing at the heavens and feeling the hum beneath her feet. The cycle continued, eternal and patient, demanding respect and vigilance. She raised her sickle to the sky, a silent vow to uphold the balance, to guide the village, and to honor the reaping in all its mystery and power. The first sunrise had marked the beginning, the second fissure had tested her resolve, and now she understood that each day, each cut of wheat, each whisper of the land, was a part of something far greater than herself—a cycle that required courage, wisdom, and unwavering attention.

Mara remained in the fields long into the night, listening, feeling, learning. The villagers had returned home, trusting her guidance, and the rider had vanished into the shadows beyond the horizon, leaving only the memory of his presence. The land was quiet now, the energy gentle and steady, but Mara knew that the reaping was not done. She could feel it, a faint pulse beneath her feet, a whisper in the wheat, a promise and a warning that tomorrow would demand her full attention once more. And Mara, hands gripping her sickle, heart steady, and mind clear, was ready to face it.

5

Chapter 5

The dawn came slowly, spilling soft orange light across the horizon and painting the edges of the wheat in molten gold. Mara rose early, before the villagers, sensing the subtle hum beneath the earth that had become her guide, her constant companion. The first sunrise had awakened her to the cycle of the reaping, the night had taught her its rhythm, and the day before had tested her resolve. Today, she would lead the village through a challenge unlike any they had faced yet—a test that would measure not only their skill but their unity, their trust, and their willingness to follow the pulse of the land.

The villagers gathered in the square, silent but expectant. Eyes wide, hands gripping tools and baskets, they waited for Mara's direction. She felt the familiar vibration beneath her feet, rising and falling like the steady beat of a drum, the earth's own rhythm guiding her movements. Her father stood beside her, pride and concern etched into his features, while the edges of the village remained quiet, the fields stretching beyond like a vast sea of gold. Mara lifted her hand, signaling the start. "Today," she said, voice steady, carrying over the whispering wind, "we move together. Trust the rhythm. Follow the pulse. Honor the harvest."

The villagers nodded, murmuring agreements and prayers under their breath. Mara led them into the fields, walking slowly, allowing the hum beneath the soil to guide her steps. Each movement was deliberate, each cut of the sickle synchronized with the pulse she felt in her chest. The wheat responded, swaying gently, almost curiously, as though testing the intentions of those who worked within it. The first fissure had been a teacher, the second a test, and now the full challenge of the harvest awaited. Mara sensed it—the land was preparing, building its energy, waiting to see if they were worthy of its gift.

Hours passed with methodical labor. The villagers' movements became more fluid under Mara's guidance, each cut precise, each stroke respectful of the life it ended. The hum beneath their feet rose and fell, a conversation between them and the soil, a song of growth and decay, of balance and consequence. Mara walked among them, adjusting stances, guiding hands, offering encouragement and quiet correction. She could feel their hesitation, their fear, but also their determination, and it filled her with a fierce pride. They were learning to read the pulse, to hear the whispers of the wheat, to participate in the cycle as it demanded.

Midday came, and the sun hung high, relentless and bright, casting the field in stark light. Mara paused for a moment, feeling the pull of energy from the earth grow stronger, different from the first two days. This was not merely the land's pulse—

it was a challenge calling for focus, unity, and courage. She knelt beside a patch of wheat that bent strangely, almost as though it resisted the rhythm, and placed her hands on the stalks. Images flashed in her mind: shadows among the wheat, villagers faltering, the harvest disrupted, life and death thrown out of balance. She pulled back, heart hammering, but quickly refocused, drawing a deep breath and centering herself in the rhythm she had learned.

A rustling sound came from the edge of the field. Mara's head snapped up. Figures emerged slowly from the boundary where the second fissure had appeared, shadows against the bright sun. They moved differently from the last time, more deliberate, more challenging, circling the villagers, testing their focus. Mara rose to her feet, placing herself between the shadows and the villagers. The rider appeared again, his presence calm but commanding, horse barely touching the earth. "They test not only skill," he said, voice low but clear. "They test unity, courage, and understanding. You must guide them. The land has chosen you to ensure balance."

Mara nodded, feeling the energy surge in her veins. She raised her sickle, not in aggression but as a symbol of participation, acknowledgment, and command. The shadows moved closer, and Mara felt the hum of the earth intensify, synchronizing with her heartbeat, guiding her steps. She signaled the villagers to follow her movements, and together they shifted, adapting to the subtle flow, cutting the wheat in patterns that mirrored the rhythm of the land. The shadows paused, then adjusted, circling with increasing complexity, forcing the villagers to anticipate and respond. Mara's hands ached, her body strained, but the pulse beneath her feet kept her grounded, kept her focused.

Hours became a blur of motion and concentration. Mara could feel the villagers' confidence growing, their movements synchronizing not only with her guidance but with the pulse of the land itself. Each shadow tested a different aspect of their skill—coordination, timing, awareness, and respect. Mara realized that the challenge was teaching them to act as one, to read the subtle cues of the earth, and to maintain harmony under pressure. She moved among them, correcting angles, adjusting timing, whispering encouragement, her own focus unwavering even as sweat dampened her brow.

By late afternoon, the shadows began to withdraw, sensing the growing harmony of the villagers' movements, the strength of their unity. Mara's chest ached with exhaustion, but she felt a quiet satisfaction settle over her. The villagers had not only performed the work of the harvest—they had participated fully in the rhythm of the land, honoring the cycle as it demanded. The hum beneath their feet softened, the whispers of the wheat became gentle, approving murmurs, and the light from the fissure diminished, leaving only the golden glow of the late afternoon sun.

Mara knelt in the center of the field, placing her hands on the soil. The pulse beneath her fingers was steady now, calm, acknowledging the success of the day. The figures that had risen from the edge of the field were gone, absorbed back into the energy of the land, leaving only memory and a faint shimmer in the distance. She felt the land's energy settle within her, a quiet resonance that would guide her through the evening and the days to come. Her father approached, placing a hand on her shoulder. "You have done more than lead," he said softly. "You have taught them to feel, to understand, to honor. The reaping is not merely a task—it is communion, and today, you have shown them the way."

The villagers gathered around Mara as the sun dipped toward the horizon, their faces reflecting fatigue, relief, and awe. Some whispered thanks, others simply watched her with a quiet reverence, sensing the magnitude of what had occurred. Mara stood slowly, letting the exhaustion weigh on her, and lifted her sickle once more. "The harvest is a cycle," she said, voice carrying over the rustling wheat. "It demands respect, focus, and unity. We have honored it today, and the land will continue to guide us. Remember this rhythm. Follow the pulse. Trust in the cycle."

As night fell, the village settled into quiet routines, families returning to their homes, fires flickering in windows, and the soft murmur of evening prayers filling the air. Mara walked through the fields one last time, hands brushing against the wheat, feeling its gentle sway, listening to its whispers. The pulse beneath her feet was steady, a reminder that the land's power was constant and eternal, patient and watchful. She understood now that the reaping was ongoing, a cycle that required vigilance, understanding, and respect, and that her role was to guide, to teach, and to honor it with every action.

The rider reappeared at the edge of the fields, silent and commanding, observing the village from a distance. Mara glanced toward him, and he inclined his head once, a gesture of approval, before melting back into the shadows. The first sunrise had awakened her, the night had trained her, the day had tested her, and the evening offered quiet reflection. She felt a connection not only to the land but to the unseen forces that governed it, an awareness that her life, her village, and the rhythm of the harvest were intertwined in ways she was only beginning to comprehend.

Mara returned to her home, heart still racing from the day's events, body exhausted but alert. She sat beside her father, recounting the moments in fragments, sharing the lessons and the sensations, the rhythm and the pulse, the challenges and the triumphs. He listened quietly, nodding, understanding more than she could articulate, his presence grounding her even as the energy of the land pulsed faintly beneath her skin. The village slept around them, trusting Mara's guidance, secure in the knowledge that the reaping had been honored, for now, and that the balance of life and harvest remained intact.

Night deepened, and Mara walked once more to the edge of the fields. Stars glittered above, indifferent and eternal, while the wheat swayed gently beneath the moonlight. She felt the pulse beneath her feet, steady and calm, a silent reminder that the cycle continued, and that each sunrise would bring new challenges, new tests, and new opportunities to honor the harvest. She raised her sickle to the sky, a silent vow to uphold the rhythm, to guide the village, and to respect the power of the land.

Mara remained in the fields long into the night, listening, feeling, learning. The village slept peacefully, confident in her guidance, while the rider watched from the shadows beyond the horizon, a guardian of the cycle and a reminder that the unseen forces of the reaping were ever-present, patient, and vigilant. The land hummed softly beneath her feet, the whispers of the wheat encouraging her, and Mara knew that tomorrow would demand her full attention once more. She felt fear, determination, and anticipation coiling within her, tempered by the knowledge that the rhythm, the pulse, and the cycle would guide her steps, her hands, and her heart.

The first sunrise had awakened her to the cycle. The second fissure had tested her resolve. Today, the village had learned to move in harmony with the pulse of the land. Mara understood, with a clarity that resonated deep in her soul, that the reaping was more than harvest—it was communion, responsibility, and awakening. She tightened her grip on the sickle, heart steady, mind clear, and prepared herself for whatever the land demanded next, ready to honor the rhythm, follow the pulse, and guide the village through the ever-turning cycle of life, death, and harvest.

6

Chapter 6

The morning air was thick with dew, the fields glistening under the soft light of dawn. Mara moved through the rows of wheat with the quiet confidence that had become second nature to her, the hum of the earth beneath her feet guiding every step, every cut of the sickle. The villagers followed, their movements synchronized not only with hers but with the pulse that seemed to flow through the land itself. The past days had tested them, taught them, and unified them, and Mara could feel the subtle change in their confidence. They were no longer tentative observers of the harvest; they were participants, attuned to the rhythm that governed life and growth.

The second fissure had closed, but its energy lingered, leaving a faint hum that whispered beneath the soil. Mara paused at its edge, resting a hand on the earth, feeling the pulse that had become her guide. Images flashed through her mind: faces of villagers past, hands shaping the fields, cycles of planting and reaping that spanned generations. She understood now that the reaping was not simply about gathering the harvest; it was about balance, awareness, and the acknowledgment of forces beyond immediate perception. The land demanded respect, and in return, it offered insight, guidance, and a connection that bound the villagers to it and to each other.

Her father appeared at her side, his presence a grounding force. "The rhythm grows stronger," he said softly, voice carrying a mixture of awe and caution. "The land acknowledges your guidance, Mara. But with recognition comes responsibility. The cycle is patient, but it watches closely." Mara nodded, sensing the weight of his words. She had learned the rhythm, but the pulse of the land was vast, its demands ongoing and ever-changing. Today, it would test them in new ways.

A sudden shift in the wind caught her attention. The wheat bent in unusual patterns, and a faint shimmer appeared at the far edge of the field, a ripple in the golden sea. Mara's heart tightened. Another fissure, smaller than the previous ones, was forming, its glow subtle but unmistakable. She turned to the villagers, who were already noticing the change, their faces reflecting a mixture of awe and apprehension. "Stay calm," she called, voice steady. "Trust the rhythm. Follow the pulse. This is part of the cycle. We move together."

The villagers nodded, adjusting their positions, hands gripping tools with renewed focus. Mara approached the shimmering fissure, feeling the hum intensify beneath her feet. This fissure was different from the last; its energy was sharper, more insistent, and it carried a sense of urgency. Shadows moved within the glow, rising slowly, testing the awareness of those who worked the fields. Mara raised her sickle, not in aggression but as an acknowledgment, a statement of participation and guidance. She could feel the energy of the fissure interacting with her own, intertwining, demanding focus, understanding, and respect.

The rider appeared silently at her side, his horse stepping lightly over the soil. "The cycle demands more than skill today," he said, voice low but commanding. "It demands awareness, unity, and courage. The fissure will not challenge you alone; it tests the village, their ability to act in harmony with the pulse of the land." Mara nodded, feeling the surge of energy in her veins. She turned to the villagers, signaling them to follow her movements. Together, they approached the fissure, hands hovering over the wheat, sensing the subtle vibrations, the whispers of the soil, the energy that demanded their attention.

The shadows within the fissure solidified, figures both ethereal and formidable, moving in patterns that tested coordination, timing, and awareness. Mara guided the villagers, adjusting their angles, timing, and strokes, helping them to respond to the subtle shifts in the energy around them. The hum beneath their feet rose and fell, synchronizing their movements, guiding their hands, and teaching them to anticipate the rhythm of the land. Sweat dampened Mara's brow, her muscles ached, but the focus in her mind was sharp, steady, and unwavering.

Hours passed in concentrated labor. Mara moved fluidly among the villagers, correcting errors, encouraging precise movements, and reinforcing the understanding that the reaping was a cycle of awareness and respect. The shadows tested them relentlessly, probing weaknesses, challenging synchronization, and demanding unity. Mara felt the villagers' confidence grow with each successful response, their movements becoming more instinctive, more attuned to the pulse that guided them. The fissure glowed brighter at moments of tension, dimming as harmony returned, as if the land itself were responding to their understanding.

By midday, the challenge intensified. The shadows shifted faster, moved in unpredictable patterns, and the fissure's glow pulsed with urgency. Mara's heart raced, but she remained calm, guiding the villagers through complex sequences of movement, teaching them to read subtle cues from the soil, the wheat, and each other. They were learning to act as one, to respond not only to her guidance but to the rhythm that flowed through the land, to anticipate shifts and challenges without hesitation. Mara could feel the energy of the fissure resonating with her own, a dialogue of pulse and response, teaching her as much as it tested her.

The villagers' synchronization improved, their confidence evident in every movement. Mara felt the hum beneath her feet become a steady current, a song of unity and understanding. The shadows, sensing the growing harmony, began to withdraw, circling slower, testing patience rather than skill. Mara's chest ached with exhaustion, but a profound satisfaction settled within her. They had met the challenge not only with skill but with awareness, respect, and unity. The fissure's glow dimmed, leaving only a faint shimmer in the golden light of the afternoon sun.

Mara knelt in the center of the field, placing her hands on the soil.

41

The pulse beneath her fingers was steady, calm, acknowledging the village's success and the completion of this stage of the cycle. The shadows faded entirely, absorbed back into the energy of the land, leaving only memory and a faint ripple in the wheat. She felt the land's energy settle within her, a quiet resonance that would guide her through the evening and the days to come. Her father approached, placing a hand on her shoulder. "You have led them well," he said softly. "Not only through labor but through understanding. Today, they have learned to move as one, to honor the cycle fully."

The villagers gathered around Mara, faces reflecting fatigue, relief, and awe. Some whispered thanks, others simply watched her with quiet reverence. Mara stood, letting the exhaustion weigh on her, and raised her sickle. "The harvest is not just about gathering," she said, voice carrying over the whispering wheat. "It is about balance, awareness, and unity. We have honored it today. Remember the rhythm, follow the pulse, and trust in the cycle."

As night fell, the village settled into quiet routines, families returning to their homes, fires flickering in windows, and the soft murmur of evening prayers filling the air. Mara walked through the fields once more, brushing her hands over the wheat, feeling the gentle sway, listening to the whispers of the land. The pulse beneath her feet was steady, a reminder that the cycle was eternal, patient, and watchful. She understood now that the reaping was ongoing, a test of vigilance, understanding, and respect, and that her role was to guide, teach, and honor it with every action.

The rider appeared one last time, watching from the edge of the fields. Mara glanced toward him, and he inclined his head in acknowledgment before disappearing into the shadows. The first sunrise had awakened her, the second fissure had tested her resolve, the challenges of the day had unified the village, and the evening offered reflection and understanding. She felt a connection not only to the land but to the unseen forces that governed it, an awareness that her life, her village, and the rhythm of the harvest were intertwined in ways she was only beginning to comprehend.

Mara returned to her home, heart still racing from the events of the day, body exhausted but alert. She recounted the moments in fragments to her father, sharing the lessons, sensations, rhythm, and pulse. He listened quietly, nodding, understanding more than she could articulate. The village slept around them, confident in her guidance, the balance of life and harvest intact for now.

Night deepened, and Mara walked to the edge of the fields, stars glittering above with indifferent beauty, while the wheat swayed gently beneath the moonlight. She felt the pulse beneath her feet, steady and calm, a silent reminder that the cycle continued, and that each sunrise would bring new challenges and tests. She tightened her grip on her sickle, heart steady, mind clear, and prepared for whatever the land demanded next, ready to honor the rhythm, follow the pulse, and guide the village through the ever-turning cycle of life, death, and harvest.

The day's challenges had revealed truths not only about the village but about Mara herself. She was no longer merely a participant in the reaping; she had become a guardian, a guide, a link between the villagers and the unseen forces of the land. Each movement, each cut, each rhythm was a lesson in understanding, a test of awareness, and a testament to the harmony possible when life, labor, and the cycle were respected. The first sunrise had awakened her, the fissures had tested her resolve, and today, she had strengthened the bond between her people and the land. Mara felt a quiet determination settle in her chest, a readiness to face whatever the next day of the harvest would demand.

The reaping was more than wheat. It was communion. It was responsibility. It was awakening. Mara stood in the fields long into the night, listening, feeling, and learning, knowing that the pulse beneath her feet and the rhythm of the land would guide her through every sunrise to come, and that the cycle was eternal, patient, and ever-watchful.

7

Chapter 7

The first light of dawn broke across the fields with a quiet intensity, spilling amber over the wheat and igniting the dew like scattered diamonds. Mara stood at the edge of the fields, the hum beneath her feet rising faintly, threading through her veins and anchoring her to the rhythm she had come to trust. The villagers had gathered behind her, eyes wide with anticipation and an unspoken tension. The past days had taught them much—the first fissure had awakened their understanding, the second had tested their resolve, and the third had unified them—but today Mara sensed the land itself demanded more, a challenge that would push beyond skill and harmony into courage and instinct.

She raised her hand, and the murmurs of the villagers fell into silence. "The cycle continues," she said, voice steady yet carrying over the field like a bell. "The land watches us. We honor it not by haste, but by understanding. Follow the pulse. Trust the rhythm. Work as one." Her words seemed to stir the wheat itself; the golden stalks swayed and whispered in response, as if acknowledging her guidance. The villagers adjusted their grips, squared their shoulders, and followed her into the field, their movements already beginning to synchronize with the subtle vibration beneath the soil.

The sun climbed steadily, casting sharp shadows across the fields. Mara's eyes were drawn to the edge where the fourth fissure was forming, thin and almost ethereal at first, but its glow intensified quickly, shimmering like molten gold as it pulsed with a rhythm entirely its own. Shadows moved within the fissure, fluid and unpredictable, coalescing into forms that were neither human nor entirely spectral. Mara felt a tension coil in her stomach—the energy was stronger, more insistent, and this time, the fissure was aware not only of her presence but of the villagers' attention as well. She could sense their unease, their hesitancy, and she knew that their fear would need to be guided, tempered with focus.

The rider appeared silently at the far edge of the field, as if emerging from the earth itself. His horse's hooves made no sound, and he observed the fissure with an intensity that Mara could feel even from a distance. "This challenge," he said, voice low but carrying a weight that demanded attention, "is unlike the others. It will test not only skill and unity, but courage, foresight, and trust. You are their guide, Mara. Lead them wisely, or the land may reject hesitation." Mara nodded, heart hammering. She gripped her sickle firmly and stepped forward, letting the pulse beneath her feet anchor her, steady her, and guide her movements.

The shadows in the fissure began to shift, flowing outwards

46

in intricate patterns that seemed almost impossible to follow. Mara lifted her hands, signaling the villagers to adjust, to respond not with force but with awareness. The hum beneath their feet rose, vibrating in sync with the fissure's glow. She moved among them, whispering directions, adjusting stances, and guiding their timing. The wheat bent and swayed around them, responding to the collective rhythm, and for a moment Mara felt as though the land itself were breathing alongside them, alive and conscious in a way that transcended comprehension.

Hours passed in a blur of motion, concentration, and unspoken communication. Mara felt the energy of the fissure probing, testing the limits of her understanding and patience. The shadows darted unpredictably, forcing the villagers to anticipate, to read cues not only from Mara but from the pulse of the land and the subtle shifts in the wheat around them. Sweat streamed down faces, hands ached from constant adjustment, and yet the rhythm persisted, guiding them, connecting them to one another and to the cycle they served. Mara herself felt the strain in her muscles, the tension in her mind, yet she remained centered, allowing instinct and understanding to drive her actions.

A sudden gust of wind swept through the field, sending ripples across the wheat. Mara froze, sensing a change in the fissure's energy—a subtle but unmistakable shift that signaled an escalation. The shadows within the glow multiplied, swirling faster, moving with increasing complexity. Mara turned to the villagers, eyes scanning their faces. Fear flickered in their expressions, but she caught their determination, the willingness to follow her lead despite uncertainty. She raised her voice, cutting through the hum and the whisper of the wheat. "Do not falter! Trust the rhythm! Follow the pulse! Act together, and the land will guide you!"

The villagers responded, their movements becoming more confident, more instinctive. Mara adjusted their positions, timing, and angles, weaving their actions into a coherent dance with the fissure's ever-shifting forms. The hum beneath their feet surged, a song of energy that resonated with every stroke of the sickle, every step in the soil. Mara felt the connection deepen, a current of understanding flowing through her and radiating to the villagers. They were learning, not just to follow her guidance, but to read the land, anticipate its cues, and move as one entity in harmony with the pulse.

By midday, the fissure's glow reached its zenith, sharp and blinding, casting golden reflections across the wheat. Mara felt the pressure in her chest, a reminder that the land demanded complete awareness. The shadows tested not only coordination but judgment, splitting and recombining unpredictably, forcing the villagers to make split-second decisions that required intuition, trust, and courage. Mara moved among them, encouraging, correcting, and sometimes stepping into the line of energy herself to demonstrate the rhythm, the balance, the respect required.

Time became fluid, measured not in hours but in the cadence of the cycle. The villagers' synchronization improved, their confidence evident in the precision and fluidity of their movements. Mara felt the fissure's energy responding, pulsating less aggressively, acknowledging their progress. The shadows slowed their motion, circling in patterns that tested patience rather than speed. Mara's chest ached, her muscles screamed in protest, yet a sense of satisfaction began to settle within her. They were meeting the challenge not only with skill but with courage, awareness, and unity.

By late afternoon, the fissure began to contract, its glow fading to a gentle shimmer, and the shadows receded, absorbed back into the energy of the land. Mara knelt in the center of the field, hands pressed into the warm soil. The pulse beneath her fingers was calm, steady, and affirming. She felt a resonance that confirmed the village had met the challenge fully, and the energy settled around them like a protective embrace. Her father approached, placing a hand lightly on her shoulder. "You have guided them well," he said quietly. "Not only through skill but through courage and understanding. The village has grown today, united in a way that the cycle recognizes."

The villagers gathered around Mara, faces reflecting exhaustion, relief, and quiet pride. Some whispered thanks, others simply looked to her with reverence. Mara stood, letting fatigue press against her body, and raised her sickle in a gesture of acknowledgment and respect. "The harvest is a cycle," she said, voice firm yet gentle. "It demands focus, awareness, courage, and unity. Today, we have honored it together. Remember the rhythm, follow the pulse, and trust in the land."

As the sun dipped toward the horizon, casting long shadows across the fields, Mara walked slowly among the wheat, brushing her hands over the stalks and listening to their soft whisper. The pulse beneath her feet was steady, a reminder that the cycle continued, patient and eternal, watching, waiting, and guiding. She understood now that the reaping was ongoing, a test of vigilance, understanding, and courage, and that her role was to lead, teach, and honor it with every action.

The rider reappeared silently at the edge of the field, watching the village from the distance. Mara glanced toward him, and he inclined his head once, a gesture of approval, before disappearing again into the shadows. The first sunrise had awakened her, the second fissure had tested her resolve, the third had unified the village, and today's challenge had demanded courage, instinct, and trust. Mara felt a connection not only to the land but to the unseen forces that governed it, an awareness that life, the village, and the rhythm of the harvest were intertwined in ways she was only beginning to comprehend.

Night deepened, and Mara returned to her home, heart still racing from the day's exertions, body exhausted but alert. She recounted the day's events in fragments to her father, sharing lessons, sensations, rhythm, and pulse. He listened quietly, nodding, understanding more than words could convey. The village slept around them, confident in Mara's guidance, their connection to the cycle strengthened, and the balance of life and harvest maintained for now.

Stars glittered overhead, indifferent yet eternal, while the wheat swayed softly beneath the moonlight. Mara stood once more at the edge of the field, feeling the pulse beneath her feet, steady and calm. Each sunrise would bring new challenges, new tests, and new lessons, and she tightened her grip on her sickle, heart steady, mind focused, ready to honor the rhythm, follow the pulse, and guide the village through the unending cycle of life, death, and harvest.

The reaping was no longer merely about wheat. It was communion, responsibility, and awakening. Mara understood fully now that her role was not only to participate but to guide, to teach, and to protect the cycle. Each day, each challenge, each pulse of the land was a lesson in understanding, balance, and respect. She remained in the fields long into the night, listening, feeling, and learning, knowing that the rhythm beneath her feet and the energy of the land would continue to guide her steps, her hands, and her heart for every sunrise yet to come.

8

Chapter 8

The morning broke with a crisp clarity, the first light spilling over the horizon and igniting the golden fields in hues of amber and copper. Mara stood at the edge of the wheat, feeling the familiar hum beneath her feet, a rhythm that pulsed like a heartbeat through the soil. Today, the village would face another challenge, one more intricate and demanding than the last. The previous fissures had awakened understanding, tested resolve, and strengthened unity, but the cycle of the reaping was relentless. Mara could sense it in the subtle vibrations of the earth, in the way the wheat bent and whispered, as if cautioning her to be both vigilant and patient.

The villagers gathered behind her, their faces a mixture of anticipation, fatigue, and determination. They had learned much in the past days, their movements now instinctively aligned with the pulse that guided Mara, and through her, they had learned to read the rhythms of the land. Mara raised her hand, calling for silence, and let her gaze sweep across the gathering. "The harvest continues," she said, voice steady and carrying across the fields. "The cycle watches us. Every step, every cut, every choice matters. Follow the pulse. Honor the rhythm. We act as one."

The wheat swayed in response, bending and shimmering as though acknowledging her words. Mara took the first step forward, her sickle held loosely in her hand, ready not to strike but to participate in the flow of energy that bound them to the land. The villagers followed, each movement synchronized, each footfall attuned to the hum beneath the soil. Today's fissure, Mara felt, would demand more than skill; it would require intuition, courage, and the willingness to confront fear without hesitation.

At the far edge of the fields, a shimmer emerged, subtle at first, then growing in intensity. The fourth fissure had already receded, leaving only faint echoes, but this new rupture pulsed with energy, sharp and insistent. Shadows rose from its center, twisting and coalescing into forms that were unpredictable and menacing, yet not entirely hostile. Mara sensed the fissure testing not just the villagers' coordination but their perception, their ability to anticipate the unseen, and their trust in her guidance.

The rider appeared silently, mounted on his spectral horse, observing the fissure and the villagers with quiet intensity. "The cycle demands awareness," he said, voice low but penetrating. "It tests courage, understanding, and the ability to act in unity. Lead them, Mara, or hesitation may undo what has been learned." Mara nodded, letting the pulse beneath her feet steady her. She could feel the villagers' tension, their anticipation, and she knew that fear would have to be guided, shaped into focus.

The fissure rippled, and shadows began to move outward in complex patterns, shifting, splitting, and reforming in ways that defied prediction. Mara stepped forward, raising her sickle in a gesture of guidance rather than defense. "Stay aware," she called, voice carrying across the field. "Trust the rhythm. Follow the pulse. Move together, act together." The villagers adjusted instantly, following her movements, allowing the pulse of the land to guide their actions. Each cut, each step, each gesture was synchronized, forming a fluid dance with the fissure's energy.

Hours passed in concentrated effort. Mara moved among the villagers, correcting positions, adjusting timing, and encouraging awareness. The shadows tested them relentlessly, probing weaknesses, challenging perception, and demanding unity. The wheat swayed and whispered, responding to their movements, to their focus, and to the understanding that the harvest was not simply an act of gathering but a communion with the land itself. Mara could feel the strain in her muscles, the tension in her mind, yet her focus remained unbroken, guided by instinct and the rhythm that had become second nature.

By midday, the fissure intensified, its glow bright and insistent. Shadows darted unpredictably, testing the villagers' ability to anticipate and respond. Mara's voice rose above the hum of the wheat. "Do not falter! Trust the rhythm! Follow the pulse! We act together, and the land will guide us!" The villagers responded, their movements flowing with increasing confidence and precision. Mara adjusted their timing and angles, weaving their actions into a coherent response to the fissure's unpredictable patterns.

The pulse beneath their feet surged in resonance with the fissure, a song of energy that connected every villager, every stalk of wheat, and Mara herself. She felt the energy of the fissure interacting with their collective awareness, each movement of the shadows prompting adjustments, anticipation, and deeper understanding. The villagers moved as one, no longer relying solely on Mara's guidance, but on the pulse that had become the unseen conductor of their actions.

By late afternoon, the fissure's energy began to ebb, its glow dimming to a soft shimmer, and the shadows receded, absorbed back into the earth. Mara knelt in the center of the field, pressing her hands into the soil. The pulse beneath her fingers was steady, calm, and affirming. She sensed the village's growth, their unity, their courage, and their understanding of the rhythm that governed the land. Her father approached, placing a reassuring hand on her shoulder. "You have guided them well," he said quietly. "Today, they have faced more than a test of skill. They have learned to act with intuition, courage, and harmony. The cycle recognizes their growth."

The villagers gathered around Mara, faces reflecting fatigue, relief, and quiet pride. Some whispered thanks, others simply looked to her with reverence. Mara rose, letting the exhaustion weigh on her, and raised her sickle. "The harvest is more than gathering," she said. "It is a communion, a responsibility, a rhythm we must honor. Today, we have acted as one. Remember the pulse, follow the rhythm, and trust in the cycle."

As the sun dipped toward the horizon, the fields glowing in the last light of day, Mara walked slowly among the wheat, brushing her hands over the stalks and listening to their whispers. The pulse beneath her feet was steady, a reminder that the cycle continued, patient, eternal, and watchful. She understood that the reaping was an ongoing process, a test of vigilance, awareness, courage, and respect, and that her role was to guide, teach, and honor it with every action.

The rider appeared once more at the edge of the field, silent and watchful. Mara glanced toward him, and he inclined his head in acknowledgment before melting into the shadows. The first sunrise had awakened her, the fissures had tested her, the challenges had unified the village, and today had demanded intuition, courage, and trust. Mara felt a connection not only to the land but to the unseen forces that governed it, an awareness that her life, her village, and the rhythm of the harvest were intertwined in ways she was only beginning to comprehend.

Night fell, and Mara returned to her home, heart racing from the exertions of the day, body exhausted but alert. She recounted the events in fragments to her father, sharing lessons, sensations, rhythm, and pulse. He listened quietly, understanding more than she could articulate. The village slept around them, confident in Mara's guidance, the balance of life and harvest maintained, and their connection to the cycle strengthened.

Stars glittered overhead, indifferent yet eternal, while the wheat swayed softly beneath the moonlight. Mara stood at the edge of the fields, feeling the pulse beneath her feet, steady and calm. She tightened her grip on her sickle, heart steady, mind focused, ready for whatever challenges awaited with the next sunrise. She understood fully now that the reaping was not merely about wheat, but about communion, responsibility, and awakening. Each day, each fissure, each pulse of the land offered lessons in awareness, balance, courage, and unity.

Mara remained in the fields long into the night, listening, feeling, and learning, knowing that the rhythm beneath her feet and the energy of the land would continue to guide her, her hands, and her heart for every sunrise yet to come. The harvest was eternal, and the cycle patient, always observing, always testing, always guiding. Mara's resolve deepened; she would meet each challenge, guide her people, and honor the rhythm of the land, for the pulse was their lifeline, and she was its chosen guardian.

9

Chapter 9

The morning sun rose slowly over the horizon, spilling molten light across the golden fields. Mara stood at the edge of the wheat, the familiar hum beneath her feet vibrating in sync with her heartbeat. Today, the rhythm of the land pulsed stronger, more insistent than before, and she felt it in every fiber of her being. The village had grown accustomed to the fissures, the challenges, the tests of skill, courage, and unity, but Mara knew that today was different. The land was restless, its energy taut and expectant. She could feel it waiting, watching, demanding something more profound than any task they had yet faced.

The villagers gathered behind her, silent but tense. They had learned the rhythms, the pulses, the ways to move in harmony with the land, but fear lingered, subtle and insidious, in their eyes. Mara raised her hand, drawing their attention. "The cycle continues," she said, voice firm yet calm. "We have faced fissures, shadows, and tests. Today, the land demands more. Focus, courage, and unity. Follow the pulse, honor the rhythm, and move as one."

The wheat swayed gently, as if acknowledging her words. Mara took a deep breath and stepped into the field, her sickle held loosely, ready to participate in the flow rather than confront it. The villagers followed, each step measured, synchronized to the hum beneath the soil. Mara felt the pulse strengthen, a current that threaded through the fields, through her, through every villager, binding them together in an unspoken understanding.

The fissure appeared at the far edge of the field, shimmering faintly at first, then growing, its glow sharp and demanding. Shadows rose from its depths, twisting and coalescing into forms both familiar and strange, their movements unpredictable, testing awareness, anticipation, and composure. Mara's heart quickened, not with fear but with focus. The villagers sensed the change as well, adjusting their stances, their hands gripping tools, their bodies tensed with readiness.

The rider appeared silently at the edge of the field, mounted on his spectral horse. His gaze swept over the fissure, the villagers, and Mara herself. "The cycle tests not only skill and courage," he said, voice low and resonant. "It tests intuition, foresight, and the ability to act in unity. Lead wisely, Mara, or hesitation may unravel what has been learned." Mara nodded, feeling the pulse beneath her feet steady her. She could sense the villagers' tension, the undercurrent of fear and anticipation, and she knew that their focus would need guidance, their courage tempered by trust.

The fissure pulsed, and the shadows began to move outward in intricate, unpredictable patterns. Mara raised her sickle, not in aggression but as a gesture of guidance, participation, and leadership. "Stay aware!" she called, voice carrying across the field. "Follow the pulse! Trust the rhythm! We act together, move together, and the land will guide us!" The villagers responded immediately, their movements flowing in sync with Mara's guidance and the pulse of the earth beneath them. Each cut, each step, each gesture was deliberate, precise, forming a fluid dance with the fissure's energy.

Hours passed in concentrated effort. Mara moved among the villagers, correcting positions, adjusting timing, and guiding their awareness. The shadows tested relentlessly, probing weaknesses, forcing anticipation, and demanding unity. The wheat bent and whispered, responding to every movement, to every adjustment, to the understanding that the harvest was not a mere task of gathering but a communion with the living land. Mara felt the strain in her muscles, the tension in her mind, yet she remained centered, guided by instinct and the rhythm that had become second nature.

By midday, the fissure intensified, its glow sharp and blinding, casting long, molten reflections across the field. Shadows darted unpredictably, testing anticipation, coordination, and trust. Mara's voice rose above the hum of the wheat. "Do not falter! Trust the rhythm! Follow the pulse! We act as one!" The villagers responded with growing confidence, their movements fluid, instinctive, and precise. Mara adjusted timing, angles, and positions, weaving their actions into a coherent response to the fissure's chaotic patterns.

The pulse beneath their feet surged in resonance with the fissure, a song of energy connecting every villager, every stalk of wheat, and Mara herself. She felt the fissure's energy interacting with their collective awareness, each movement prompting adjustments, anticipation, and deeper understanding. The villagers moved as one, relying not only on Mara's guidance but on the pulse that had become their unseen conductor.

A sudden wind swept through the field, stirring the wheat into a frenzy. Mara paused, sensing a shift in the fissure's energy, a spike in intensity that signaled escalation. The shadows moved faster, more complex, splitting and recombining unpredictably. Mara turned to the villagers, reading their faces. Fear flickered, but determination burned brighter. She raised her voice above the growing hum. "Focus! Trust the rhythm! Follow the pulse! Together, we honor the land!"

The villagers responded, their movements merging with the pulse of the earth, guided by Mara's steady presence. Each step, each cut, each gesture flowed with increasing fluidity and precision. The fissure's shadows slowed their motion, circling with measured intent, testing patience and harmony rather than force. Mara's chest ached with exertion, but a sense of profound satisfaction settled within her. They were not only meeting the challenge with skill but with courage, awareness, and unity.

The afternoon sun blazed overhead, casting sharp light across the fields. The fissure's glow began to diminish, the shadows retreating, absorbed back into the earth. Mara knelt in the center of the field, pressing her hands into the warm soil. The pulse beneath her fingers was steady, calm, affirming. She sensed the village's growth, their unity, courage, and understanding of the rhythm governing the land. Her father approached, placing a hand on her shoulder. "You have guided them well," he said quietly. "Today, they have faced more than skill—they have acted with intuition, courage, and harmony. The cycle recognizes their growth."

The villagers gathered around Mara, faces reflecting exhaustion, relief, and pride. Some whispered thanks, others looked with reverence. Mara rose, letting fatigue press against her body, and lifted her sickle. "The harvest is more than gathering," she said. "It is communion, responsibility, and rhythm. Today, we acted as one. Remember the pulse, follow the rhythm, and trust the cycle."

As the sun dipped below the horizon, casting long shadows over the fields, Mara walked among the wheat, brushing her hands over the stalks, listening to their soft whisper. The pulse beneath her feet remained steady, a reminder that the cycle continued, patient, eternal, and vigilant. She understood that the reaping was an ongoing process, a test of awareness, courage, and respect, and that her role was to guide, teach, and honor it with every movement.

The rider appeared again at the field's edge, silent and watchful. Mara met his gaze, and he inclined his head in acknowledgment before fading into the shadows. The first sunrise had awakened her, the fissures had tested her resolve, the challenges had unified the village, and today had demanded intuition, courage, and trust. Mara felt the connection deepen—not only to the land but to the unseen forces that governed it, an awareness that life, the village, and the rhythm of the harvest were intertwined in ways she was only beginning to comprehend.

Night fell, and Mara returned home, heart racing from the exertions, body exhausted but alert. She recounted the day's events to her father, sharing fragments of rhythm, pulse, and sensation. He listened quietly, nodding, understanding more than words could convey. The village slept around them, confident in Mara's guidance, the balance of life and harvest maintained, their connection to the cycle strengthened.

Stars glittered above, indifferent yet eternal, while the wheat swayed softly beneath the moonlight. Mara returned to the edge of the fields, feeling the pulse beneath her feet, steady and calm. Each sunrise would bring new challenges, new tests, and new lessons. She tightened her grip on her sickle, heart steady, mind focused, prepared to honor the rhythm, follow the pulse, and guide the village through the unending cycle of life, death, and harvest.

The reaping was more than wheat. It was communion, responsibility, and awakening. Mara understood that her role was not only to participate but to guide, to teach, and to protect the cycle. Each day, each fissure, each pulse offered lessons in awareness, balance, courage, and unity. She remained in the fields long into the night, listening, feeling, learning, knowing that the rhythm beneath her feet and the energy of the land would continue to guide her hands and her heart for every sunrise yet to come.

The village had grown stronger, more confident, yet Mara knew the pulse was not static. It would continue to test them, challenge them, and demand more with every sunrise. She had learned that leadership was not about command but about connection, about reading the rhythms of the land and guiding others to move in harmony with them. The cycle was eternal, patient, and ever-watchful, and she was its chosen guardian.

Mara lifted her sickle one final time, heart steady, eyes scanning the fields under the moonlit sky. The pulse beneath her feet thrummed softly, a gentle reminder of the land's presence, its wisdom, and its expectation. She whispered a vow to the rhythm, the cycle, the harvest itself: she would honor it, guide her people, and act with courage, awareness, and unity. The fissures, the shadows, the tests—they were part of the communion, part of the awakening that defined the land and its people.

The night deepened, and Mara stood alone in the fields, listening, feeling, and learning. The rhythm of the land, the pulse beneath her feet, and the whispers of the wheat intertwined, creating a tapestry of energy that connected the past, the present, and the promise of future sunrises. Mara understood that the reaping was more than harvest—it was life itself, a cycle of constant challenge, learning, and growth. She remained vigilant, aware, and ready, knowing that the pulse of the land would always guide her, her hands, and her heart.

Chapter 10

The first rays of dawn broke over the horizon, spilling gold across the fields like molten fire. Mara stood at the edge of the wheat, the familiar pulse beneath her feet resonating stronger than ever. The cycle of the reaping had tested her, the village, and the land itself in ways she could never have anticipated, and now the final challenge awaited. The fissures had taught them skill, courage, unity, and awareness, but the last sunrise promised something more profound: a reckoning, a culmination of all the lessons, and the ultimate test of the bond between the villagers, Mara, and the land itself.

The villagers gathered behind her, faces etched with anticipation, exhaustion, and determination. They had grown under Mara's guidance, learning not only to follow but to feel the pulse, to anticipate the rhythm, to act with a unity that transcended instruction. Mara raised her hand, drawing silence across the field. "Today, the cycle reaches its peak," she said, voice firm yet resonant. "We have learned, we have grown, we have acted as one. Now, we face the final test. Follow the pulse, trust the rhythm, and honor the land."

The wheat swayed in response, a gentle whispering that seemed to carry approval. Mara stepped forward, her sickle held loosely, a symbol of participation rather than confrontation. The villagers followed, each movement precise, instinctive, and attuned to the energy that hummed through the soil. Mara felt the pulse surge beneath her feet, stronger than ever, threading through the village, connecting them as a single entity with the land and the unseen forces that governed it.

The fissure appeared at the far edge of the field, larger and more radiant than any before, pulsing with an energy that demanded attention, respect, and complete awareness. Shadows emerged, swirling and shifting, coalescing into forms that were both terrifying and mesmerizing. Mara's chest tightened—not with fear, but with focus. She sensed that this fissure would challenge everything they had learned: skill, intuition, courage, trust, and above all, unity.

The rider appeared silently at the edge of the field, his spectral horse poised and watchful. "This is the culmination," he said, voice low but penetrating. "The cycle tests not only your abilities but your understanding, your connection to the land, and your bond with one another. Lead wisely, Mara. Hesitation now could unravel all that has been achieved." Mara nodded, feeling the pulse beneath her feet steady her. She could sense the villagers' anxiety, the flickers of fear, and knew that their courage and focus would need careful guidance.

The fissure pulsed, and the shadows surged outward in intricate, unpredictable patterns, faster and more complex than any they had faced before. Mara raised her sickle, not in defense but as a gesture of guidance, a conduit for the rhythm that would unify the village. "Stay aware!" she called, voice cutting through the hum of the wheat. "Follow the pulse! Trust the rhythm! Move as one!"

The villagers responded immediately, their movements flowing with the pulse, each step, each swing of a sickle, each gesture synchronized in a dance with the fissure's energy. Mara moved among them, correcting stances, adjusting timing, and reinforcing awareness. The shadows tested relentlessly, probing weaknesses, forcing anticipation, and demanding unity. The wheat bent and whispered around them, responding to their focus and respect, a living entity in communion with those who honored the cycle.

Hours passed in concentrated effort. Mara felt the pulse intensify, a symphony of energy that threaded through every villager, every stalk of wheat, and herself. The fissure's shadows moved with greater speed and complexity, testing not only coordination but judgment and trust. Mara's voice rose above the hum. "Do not falter! Follow the rhythm! Trust the pulse! Together, we honor the land!"

The villagers' confidence grew with each synchronized movement, each anticipatory response, each gesture aligned with the rhythm of the land. Mara guided them, weaving their actions into a coherent response, but she also felt the pulse flowing into them, empowering them to act with instinct and understanding beyond instruction. The fissure's energy seemed to respond, the shadows slowing their motion, circling with measured intent, testing harmony rather than force.

By midday, the fissure reached its apex, glowing fiercely, casting molten reflections across the fields. Mara's muscles ached, her mind raced, yet her focus remained unbroken. She moved fluidly among the villagers, adjusting positions, correcting angles, encouraging intuition, and reinforcing the understanding that the harvest was more than labor—it was communion, awareness, and respect.

A sudden gust of wind swept through the field, stirring the wheat into waves of gold. Mara paused, sensing a shift in the fissure's energy—a spike in intensity that signaled escalation. The shadows multiplied, moving faster, splitting and recombining unpredictably. Mara turned to the villagers, reading their expressions. Fear flickered, but determination shone brighter. She raised her voice above the rising hum. "Focus! Trust the rhythm! Follow the pulse! Together, we act as one!"

The villagers responded with renewed vigor. Their movements merged seamlessly with the pulse of the earth, guided by Mara's steady presence and the unseen current that flowed through all of them. Each step, each cut, each gesture became instinctive, a perfect reflection of the unity that had grown between them, the bond between the village, Mara, and the land. The fissure's shadows slowed, circling as if acknowledging the harmony, testing patience and respect rather than speed or force.

By late afternoon, the fissure's energy began to wane, its glow softening, shadows dissolving, absorbed back into the earth.

Mara knelt in the center of the field, pressing her hands into the warm soil. The pulse beneath her fingers was steady, affirming. She sensed the village's growth, their courage, unity, and deep understanding of the rhythm that governed the land. Her father approached, placing a gentle hand on her shoulder. "You have led them well," he said quietly. "They have faced not only challenges of skill, but tests of intuition, trust, and harmony. The cycle recognizes your guidance, their growth, and the bond that has been strengthened."

The villagers gathered around Mara, faces glowing with pride, relief, and awe. Some whispered words of thanks, others gazed in silent reverence. Mara rose, letting the exhaustion weigh on her, and lifted her sickle. "The harvest is more than wheat," she said, voice steady, resonant. "It is communion, responsibility, and awakening. Today, we honored the cycle fully. Remember the pulse, follow the rhythm, and trust in the land."

As the sun dipped below the horizon, casting long shadows across the golden fields, Mara walked among the wheat, brushing her hands over the stalks, listening to their whispers. The pulse beneath her feet remained steady, a quiet reminder that the cycle continued, eternal and patient. She understood that the reaping was ongoing, a test of vigilance, awareness, courage, and unity, and that her role was to guide, teach, and honor it with every movement.

The rider appeared once more at the edge of the field, silent and watchful. Mara met his gaze, and he inclined his head in acknowledgment before fading into the shadows. The first sunrise had awakened her, the fissures had tested her resolve, the challenges had unified the village, and today's final test had demanded courage, intuition, and trust. Mara felt a profound connection, not only to the land but to the unseen forces that governed it, an awareness that life, the village, and the rhythm of the harvest were bound together in ways she was only beginning to comprehend.

Night fell, and Mara returned home, heart racing from the day's exertions, body exhausted but alert. She recounted the events to her father, sharing fragments of pulse, rhythm, and sensation. He listened quietly, nodding, understanding more than words could convey. The village slept around them, confident in Mara's guidance, the balance of life and harvest maintained, and their connection to the cycle stronger than ever.

Stars glittered overhead, indifferent yet eternal, while the wheat swayed softly beneath the moonlight. Mara stood at the edge of the fields, feeling the pulse beneath her feet, steady and calm. Each sunrise would bring new challenges, new tests, and new lessons, but today had shown her the power of unity, trust, and awareness. She tightened her grip on her sickle, heart steady, mind focused, prepared to honor the rhythm, follow the pulse, and guide the village through the unending cycle of life, death, and harvest.

The reaping had always been more than wheat. It was communion, responsibility, and awakening. Mara understood fully now that her role was not only to participate but to guide, to teach, and to protect the cycle. Each day, each fissure, each pulse of the land had been a lesson in awareness, balance, courage, and unity. She remained in the fields long into the night, listening, feeling, and learning, knowing that the rhythm beneath her feet and the energy of the land would continue to guide her hands, her heart, and her people for every sunrise yet to come.

The village had grown stronger, more confident, and Mara knew that the pulse was eternal. It would continue to test, challenge, and demand more with each new day. She had learned that leadership was not command but connection, that the true strength of the village lay not in individual skill but in unity, trust, and harmony with the land. The cycle was eternal, patient, and ever-watchful, and she was its chosen guardian.

Mara lifted her sickle one final time, heart steady, eyes scanning the fields under the moonlit sky. The pulse beneath her feet thrummed softly, a gentle reminder of the land's presence, its wisdom, and its expectation. She whispered a vow to the rhythm, to the cycle, to the harvest itself: she would honor it, guide her people, and act with courage, awareness, and unity. The fissures, the shadows, the tests—they were all part of the communion, part of the awakening that defined the land and its people.

The night deepened, and Mara stood alone in the fields, listening, feeling, learning. The rhythm of the land, the pulse beneath her feet, and the whispers of the wheat intertwined, creating a tapestry of energy connecting the past, the present, and the promise of future sunrises. She understood that the reaping was life itself, a cycle of constant challenge, learning, and growth. She remained vigilant, aware, and ready, knowing that the pulse of the land would always guide her, her hands, and her heart.

The first sunrise of tomorrow would bring no fissures, no

shadows, no tests. It would bring peace, understanding, and reflection. Mara allowed herself a quiet smile, a rare moment of relief and gratitude. The village had learned, grown, and united. She had led them, guided them, and taught them to trust not only her but the pulse of the land, the rhythm of life itself.

The harvest would continue, as it always had, and as it always would. Mara would remain, standing vigilant, connected, and ready. She had become not only a participant but a guardian, a bridge between the village and the eternal rhythm that sustained them. The reaping was complete for now, the cycle honored, and the bond between Mara, the villagers, and the land stronger than ever.

The night carried a serene hush over the fields. Mara lingered, hands brushing the wheat, listening to its soft whispers. She felt the pulse beneath her feet, steady, eternal, a reminder of the unity, courage, and awareness that had been forged through challenge. The fissures were gone, the shadows dissipated, but the lessons remained, etched into the land, the village, and her own being.

Mara lowered her sickle, feeling the weight of responsibility, the quiet pride in the village's growth, and the enduring pulse that connected them all. She knew that the reaping was never truly finished

—it was a cycle, patient, eternal, and vigilant. But for now, she allowed herself to breathe, to absorb the stillness, and to honor the land that had guided, tested, and taught them all.

The final chapter of the cycle had closed, the village united, and Mara stood as its guardian, heart steady, mind clear, hands ready, and spirit attuned to the rhythm of the land, prepared for all the sunrises yet to come.